One Season in Hell

in pursuit of
Arthur Rimbaud

Other publications by Michael Glover

Poetry:

Measured Lives (1994)
Impossible Horizons (1995)
A Small Modicum of Folly (1997)
The Bead-Eyed Man (1999)
Amidst All This Debris (2001)
For the Sheer Hell of Living (2008)
Only So Much (2011)
Hypothetical May Morning (2018)
Messages to Federico (2018)
What You Do With Days (2019)

Others:

Headlong into Pennilessness (2011)
Great Works: Encounters with Art (2016)
Playing Out in the Wireless Days (2017)
111 Places in Sheffield You Shouldn't Miss (2017)
Late Days (2018)
Neo Rauch (2019)
The Book of Extremities (2019)
Thrust (2019)
John Ruskin: an idiosyncratic dictionary (2019)
Rose Wylie (2020)
Whose? (2020)
The Trapper (2020)

As editor or contributor:

Memories of Duveen Brothers (1976)
Goin' down, down, down: Matthew Ronay (2006)
Between Eagles and Pioneers: Georg Baselitz (2011)
Robert Therrien (2016)
Monique Frydman (2017)

One Season in Hell

in pursuit of
Arthur Rimbaud

Michael Glover

Copyright © Michael Glover 2020
The moral rights of the author have been asserted.
Artwork © Ruth Dupré, Michael Glover and 1889 books

www.1889books.co.uk

ISBN: 978-1-9163622-2-2

for Jesse

A note about this writing

This is not a translation of *Une Saison en Enfer* (1872–3) by Arthur Rimbaud in any respectable or conventional meaning of the word. It is a *farouche* version of sorts, a riff, a homage, a seeing-through, an imitation with shameless embellishments and unfaithfulnesses, anachronistic additions and variations (think of Ezra Pound's *Homage to Sextus Propertius* if you are keen to pursue inexact parallels); an endeavour to capture the mood, the temper, the lived moment of this disaffected young man from Charleville as he reaches the end of his tumultuously brief vocation as a *poète maudit*.

Une Saison en Enfer is a wild, raving, raging and rollicking, unruly, feverish, jumpy, staccato, self-lacerating, self-contradictory, fist-shaking, puffed-out-chested, pressure-cooked-delirious and posturingly theatrical piece of free-form prose-cum-verse by a boy born into oppressive respectability who has run away from home and chosen a life on the margins of vagabondage, a boy with wild hair (Verlaine's drawing of that hair will cause a cultural revolution in its own right), in the company of a male lover, who also happens to be a great poet called Paul Verlaine. I will say almost nothing about this relationship because too much has been written and idly speculated already. Let this suffice. Yes, Verlaine shot him, and was sent to prison as a punishment, but it was only a wrist wound, as much a serious graze as anything else. And anyway, who would ever expect a poet to be a good shot? Very soon after, a fairly mediocre painter called Jef Rosman flashed off a portrait of Rimbaud on his hospital bed, looking small, self-protective, and thoroughly sorry for himself — every inch the wounded animal — because it damned well hurt, hurt, hurt for a while, didn't it?

And after the spittingly brief explosion of poetry (he had written his last poem by the age of about nineteen) comes that strange afterlife of wandering (often on foot, like a pilgrim), merchant-venturing and gun-running, in Africa and elsewhere, before cancer kills him at the age of 37.

Yes, Arthur Rimbaud, that sullen seethe of a schoolboy caught so beautifully on camera by Carjat in 1871, walked away from poetry, but that same poetry continues to go in relentless pursuit of its readers. And this piece of writing is a small contribution to our pursuit of him — and it.

Who will ever quite fathom him? Or perhaps it would be more honest to ask: who has ever truly fathomed any human being?

Summer after summer I have taken this book to France with me and, in reading and re-reading it, found myself knocking on its door without perhaps even being aware of that fact. As summer bled into autumn of 2019, the door felt slightly ajar.

Géay and London, August–October 2019

What is to become of me? Am I not to die an amputee? I died an amputee. That is my story.

In former times, if I remember it well, my life was a feast at which all hearts opened, where every wine flowed in such abundance...

Beauty, Beauty, I said to Beauty herself one sweet evening, come and sit on my knee. And I found her bitter. And I cursed her.

I took up arms against justice.

I fled from myself. Did I not award all my hard won treasures to hatred, misery and all those other malign sorcerers?

I caused all human hope to vanish from within me. To stultify every joy, I made a single, silent leap, like some ferocious beast.

When the executioners came to call (at my own request, I hasten to add), I had the gall to bite their guns, one by one, clean in two, bam bam, as I expired! I called down the plagues to make away with me with the aid of blood and sand. Unhappiness has been my deity. I stretched myself out full-length in the mud. I dried myself by time's gentle breeze. And I've done tricks enough to drive anyone to the brink of insanity.

And springtime gifted me with the grin of an idiot.

And now, on the very brink of my last gasp, I've dreamt of seizing hold once again of the key to that ancient feast, where at least I would regain my appetite.

This key goes by the name of charity. Surely such inspiration proves I have been dreaming!

'But you'll still be laughing like a hyena...' exclaims once again that demon who crowned me with poppies. 'Seize hold of death while your appetites, your egotism and all those capital sins are in full vigour.'

Ah! I'm over the top again. But, dear Satan, I beg of you for an eye less red with rage, and as I lie in wait here for all the puny acts of cowardice that will emerge later, let me tear off for you these few unpleasant pages from my notebook of damnation. Yes, let me do it for you alone, yes you, who adore in any writer the absence of gifts descriptive or instructive,...

Bad Blood

And what of my Gallic ancestry? Well now, let me see... Eyes of the palest blue edging off to grey, skull keen and narrow as a blade, with a certain clumsiness in all those knockabout games in the playground...

I'm scruffy, unkempt too – but at least I don't grease back my hair like all the other buffoons!

Pitiless flayers of their beasts, those Gauls were the very soul of ineptitude when it came to brazen, scorched-earth tactics!

I adored all their vices, eagerly inheriting them one by one: idleness, lust, anger, idolatry, but above all things else, a lavish penchant for lies, lies, lies.

Who has decapitated a saint better than I?

Perhaps it's work I hate most of all, hard graft, hand-toil involving masters and men – who needs all that crap? Who's happy to show off the broken back of a sweat-soaked peasant? Isn't it easier to push along a pen than a plough?

Join this century of slaving hands! That's what they all cry. I'm happy to give mine away. Domestic drudgery's a fool's game which never ends – ask my mother's scullery maid!

The beautiful, guileless honesty of beggars, it's that which breaks my heart. How to choose between castration and criminality? They're equally disgusting. Me? I'm still all of a piece. You just watch me...

Who made this tongue of mine so treacherous? Who guided and protected me in all my careful practice of this Religion of Idleness?

My body's good for nothing but slumming. Haven't you seen me everywhere, sporting a yawn wider than a toad's? Can you name a great family of Europe I have not hobnobbed with?

We're all families together these days, yours, mine, theirs, all preaching and speechifying of the Rights of Man... Oh, away with all this blethering...

The truth is that I'm nowhere and nothing. No one owns me. No one claims me. I come from a race as proud and as vaunted as this handful of dirt I let slip through my fingers...

Revolution means nothing to me. It's a fool's game. I drag myself out of bed only to steal — like that wolf forever taunting its prey.

O France, fairest daughter of the Church, how I embrace you, dragging my weary, humble limbs across all that sacred ground, from the Swabian plains to Byzantium in all its glory, up to the very gates of Jerusalem, where I proclaim aloud the Cult of Mary, and curse the hung bones of the crucified lord.

Like a leper, I squat amongst the shattered amphorae, all those broken stones. Then, a little later, paid and eager to kill, I'm bivouacked beneath the stars of Germany.

Good lord, what Days we have, what Hours!

When the Witch's Sabbath comes round, I'm caught in a frenzied dance with old and young, in a circle of ground that blazes red as the fire of the setting sun.

I remember nothing but this earth on which I stand, this accursed Christianity in which I'm rooted like a tree. Only the past engulfs me. But always alone. Where is my family? What language ought I to be speaking?

What was I once? I grasp only at now, now, now. No more vagabondage. No more wars swim in front of my eyes. We who have been crushed to death, we always win out in the end. Who listens to Jesus these days? How hollow ring the Counsels of the Lords!

Oh science, our supreme god! Everything's wrapped up like a pretty parcel. Everything's done and dusted. The body. The soul. We have philosophies and medicines to hand, old wives' tales, popular song... The princes are all butchered, those old Prohibitionists with their ridiculous diversions! Sing out this bold litany, boys: geography, cosmography, mechanical engineering, chemistry!

Science is the new nobility. Progress is on the march. The world runs helter-skelter. Who'd reverse all that? Why piece together shattered mirrors in the dark?

The vision of numbers, that's what we're all into these days. Let the Spirit guide us... Numbers, numbers seduce us. Just listen to these oracular words, sure as nails in a board. I understand it all. And if the heathen words won't serve, play dumb.

———

The blood of the heathen, how come it's here again though? Why hasn't Jesus second-come to aid me, letting my soul embrace Freedom and Liberty? Did the Gospel pass me by when I was nodding drunkenly beside the road?

I'm so greedy for God above, being of an inferior race to all eternity...

Here I am again on this Breton shore. Towns flare into light and life as evening falls. My day's over and done. I'm quitting Europe — and be damned to it all. It's a sick dog. Let the sea air burn my lungs. Let all those climates lost and gone weather me. To swim, hunt, smoke, trample virgin ground, drink liquor fierce as bubbling metal — just like those ancestors used to do squatted around their smoke and flames — that's me to a tee..

I'll be back again, pumped up with limbs of iron, skin dark, eye ferocious. By my mask, you will know the strength of my inheritance. I'll stagger beneath the weight of all that fool's gold. I'll be supremely idle, brutish as a dog with one eye. Women will cluck around me in all my decrepit savagery, new returned from all the coruscating heat of some oriental mystery. I'll even get involved in politics. SAVED, that's the word they'll be muttering piously, *sotto voce*.

But just now I'm in the shadow of a curse. I loathe my native country. The best thing for me would be to be slumped on a beach in a drunken blurt of vomit.

We're not leaving though. We're not about to go running scared. Let's resume walking the old roads, burdened by the usual vices, driven into our side like that spear into the sun-seared flank of the man crucified. Let me suffer for the sake of Reason, watch it rise up into the sky, and then come swooping back down before it throws me over and heaves me aside.

These last rags and tatters of innocence. My final acts of timidity. There, I've said it. Don't drag all my disgusts, all my betrayals of self and others into the world.

Let's be off then. On the march, bearing our burdens through deserts, boredom, fury.

Who am I on loan to? What foul beast waits to be adored? What holy image assails me? Whose hearts am I about to break? What lies am I nursing? Through whose blood am I to be tramping?

Be on guard against Justice. Life, so hard, so bitter, trudges along wearisomely. Brutal. Brutish. Whip off the coffin's lid with your dry, corpse-like fist. Slump down. Asphyxiate yourself if you so wish.

The end of old age has come, all dangers past. Terror becomes not the French language, ahem.

Oh, I am so fagged out, done in, that I'm giving away all my wild gesturings of perfection.

Such abnegation! Such displays of charity! Down here too, where the worms live!

De profundis Domine, what a burdensome beast of a boy/man I am...

While still a child, I was besotted by the unredeemable convict, he on whom the iron gates of incarceration would forever be slamming. I'd haunt all the inns, those stinking dens made sacred by his visitations. I even saw through his eyes the blueness of the sky, the labour in blossom throughout the countryside. I smelt his death-stink in the towns. He had more power than a saint, more good sense than the boldest voyager —

he alone was my mentor, my fellow traveller, along those paths of Reason and Glory!

On all the roads, through those long nights of winter, without a roof over my head, clothes to stand up in, or even a nub of bread to gnaw on, a voice seized hold of my frozen heart: weakness or strength, acknowledge it, that strength inside you. You know neither where you are going nor why. Poke your nose into every hole, reply to them all. No one will kill you. Who'd have the gall to butcher a corpse?

How lost I looked on those bygone mornings, dead long before my dying. Perhaps, had you seen me, you would not even have seen me...

Red, black mud of a sudden rose up in front of me in those towns, like a mirror which seeks out its likeness in some neighbouring bedroom, or a treasure trove found deep delved from some forest gloom!

Good luck! I cried out (but who heard me?). I saw a sea of flames and smoke intermingled, and, to left and to right of me, such riches pouring forth — at least the equal of a thousand thunderous rumblings...

But orgies, and even the friendship of women, were still forbidden me. Not a single companion. There I observed myself, in front of an enraged crowd, face to face with the firing squad's bristle of guns, crying over my own misery, that they of course failed to comprehend, let alone pardon! — O Joan of Arc, stand now with me!

Preachers, professors, masters of my fate, you are so wrong to put me at the mercy of so called Justice. I do not recognise these people. I have never been a Christian. I am of that race which sings its heart out on the scaffold. Your laws are meaningless to me. My moral compass is altogether shattered. I am a brute beast. Oh, how you misconstrued me!

Yes, my eyes screw tight when those blazing searchlights swing from side to side. I am a beast, a black, to my heart. And yet I can be salvaged from all this wreckage. It is you who are the fakers, the false negroes amongst us, you greedy, ravenous madmen.

Tradesman, stare at your black heart. Magistrate, you are a negro too. You too, cocksure, strutting general; and you, Emperor of us all, wildly scratching at your fleas as you guzzle your untaxed liquor, you too were fabricated in the heat and the filth of Satan's factory. How to describe your kind? Engendered by fever and cancer. The old and the ancient are so respectable that they shriek like children to be boiled alive!

Cleverest, sneakiest of all would be to steal away altogether, set sail from this accursed continent forever, where madness prowls, unceasing in its seeking out of hostages for all these wretches. Let me instead walk proud towards the real kingdom of the children of Ham.

Is Nature fathomable at all? Could I be said even to know myself?

No more words please, no more words. Let me bury the dead in my own swollen belly. Strike up with the drums. Dance, dance, dance your frenzied rounds! I cannot even foresee that hour when all the pallid spectres must disembark, and I will plunge down, down, down into nothingness.

Hunger, thirst, shouts, dance, dance, dance!

———

See how the white spectres disembark. Such a deafening cannonade! Submit yourself now to baptism, do not hesitate for a moment. Dress yourself seemly. Set yourself to work.

Floored by this blow to the heart I could never have foreseen. I have done no evil. There has been a pleasing lightness about my days. I will be spared the need for repentance. Is it my goodness which has saved me those torments of the soul, afflictions almost unto death, that light, so austere and so holy, which dithers behind the funeral candles?

This is the fate of the family's favourite son, the anointed one. The coffin slides in too soon, soaked by such limpid tears. Let me not deny it then: debauchery is folly, vice the habit of beasts. Cast yourself off from all corruption! It is not merely the doleful hour of sorrow that the clock will not have sounded. Am I to be snatched away like a child, playing his games of forgetfulness beyond the skies?

Quickly now! Are there not other lives to be fathomed? Sleep amidst such riches, such abundance, has to be nonsense.. Only Divine Love, excelling all others, can wield the keys of Science. Nature is nothing but an extravagant blazing forth of goodness. Goodbye then, all chimerical nonsense, ideals, errors...

The song of angels, in sweet harmony of reason, rises from the lifeboat. This is love divine, I tell you. Love twice over — and over. Let me die of my devotion to this terrestrial love, oh let me. See these souls that I have left behind. Their pain will increase, the further I recede. You are choosing me from all these shipwrecked survivors. Are not those who remain my friends? Save them then, save them...

Reason came to birth within me. The world is good and wholesome. I shall bless this life. These are no longer the promises of a child. Neither to escape from old age, nor from death once so certain. It is God who fills me with his strength, it is He alone that I must be praising.

Tedium, I no longer embrace you as my beloved. All those outbursts of anger, debauchery, sheer stupidity — the sheer burden of it all is shrugged off. Let us savour instead the broad-based bountifulness of my innocence...

A bastinado! Who but a fool would take comfort in that? I am under no illusion that I am setting sail for my nuptials with Jesus himself cast in the role of the bride's father.

No, Reason has not taken me prisoner. I have said the one word: God. I crave the two-in-one: freedom and salvation. But how to achieve it? All frivolous tastes have bade me adieu, adieu. Do I even need devotion, divine love? I don't regret that century when all hearts seemed to possess a unique sensitivity. Everyone has reasons of his own to embrace scorn or charity: I keep my place at the summit of this angelic ladder of good sense.

As for happiness long established, domestic or otherwise... no, I simply cannot hack it. I'm too feeble, too all over the place... According to the old saw, life flourishes by virtue of work. As for myself, my life is not enough of a burden. It flees, flies away, idly afloat way above the action, that hallowed place where all the sweetly virtuous gather like hens mother-clucking...

What an old woman I have become, lacking the courage to love death!

Oh if only God would bless me with calmness celestial, aerial, or even the gift of prayer — just like those old saints — the saints! Such men of strength! The anchorites, a type of the artist with which we have now dispensed.

Farce everlasting. My innocence should make me weep. Farce is the game we all must play. Your go.

———

Enough of it all! Punishment enough! On the march we go...

Ah! How my lungs burn, my temples thunder. Night rolls around my eyes, mediated by this dazzle of sunlight. My heart! My limbs!

Where to go? Into battle? I am so weak. Others are about to storm me. Tools, arms — at such an hour as this one...

Fire! Fire rains down on me. There, where I am due. Cowards! I must kill myself, fall at the feet of horses. Ah! ... I'll grow accustomed to it all.

Let us call it the French way of life, the pathway of honour!

Night of Hell

So I gulped down the poison. Thrice blessed be my counsellor! My guts burn. The venom, its consuming violence, pulls my limbs awry, drags me earthward. I am dying of thirst, suffocating, I cannot even cry out. Hell is within me, pains unending. See how the flames rear! I burn as I must. Get thee gone, Demon!

I had even foreseen my conversion to well-being, contentment, salvation. The vision rises. Hell will not countenance hymns of adoration. Thousands of creatures, so charming, so seductive, a concert of voices so suavely gliding, strength, peace, noble ambition, who knows?

Noble ambitions!

The vividness of life as it is! But what if damnation exists for all eternity? A man who scourges himself is damned, surely? If I believe myself in hell, there I am, surely? It is the Catechism fulfilling its own words. I am a slave to those Baptismal vows. Parents, it is you who have created my unhappiness — and yours too. Poor innocent child! Hell cannot attack pagans. Life is still here, in all its vividness! Later, the sweetness of damnation will be that much more deep-grounded... The crime, pronounced in a flash, is that I am destined to fall into nothingness. Human law has said so.

Silence! Be silent! Here is all shame, all reproof: Satan himself, he who tells us that fire is ignoble, my anger frightful and stupid. Enough of all this! The whisperings of my errors, tricks of the old trade, those perfumes which reek, a child's plink-plonks on the piano.

And to have affirmed, so outrageously, that I am at one with the truth, that I stare justice in the eye: my judgement is sane and steady, I am ripe now for perfection...Such pride! My skull's very skin shrivels and shrinks. Pity me! Lord, I am so afraid. I am consumed by such thirst, such thirst!

Ah, childhood, the grasses, the rain, lake water running over the stones, by the light of the moon when the bell tolls noon...The Devil's in the belfry at such an hour. Mary! Blessed Saint and Virgin! I live in horror of my own beastliness...

Over there, are not good, honest souls wishing me well? Come see... The pillow lies across my mouth. They cannot hear me, all those phantoms. Then again, no one gives a toss about other people. Forbid them to approach. I smell burning, surely approaching.

Hallucinations crowd about me, unbending. Things are as they have always been: no faith in history, all principles lost and forgotten. I shall be silent: poets and visionaries would be far too jealous. I am a thousandfold the richer for it, let us all be greedy kin of the engulfing depths of the sea.

Listen out, ye wantons! The clock has just come to a dead stop. I am out of this world altogether. Theology really means something!

Hell is below us for sure, heaven high as the sky. Ecstasy, nightmare, and all roiling in a nest of flames...

My ears are pricked to those nasty tricksters in the countryside... Satan, Ferdinand, flashing through the corn like serpents... Jesus walking tall upon the unbending briars, Jesus barely ruffling the surface of the waters. The lantern showed him to us: pale skin; brown, streaming tresses; side profile a vague emerald in hue...

Prestidigitator supreme, I quick-yank the cloth off all the mysteries: religious or of this world; death, birth, future, past; from cosmogony to Nothingness. I am the master of all phantasmagoria.

Listen!

I possess every talent known to man. No one's here. There's also someone, I sense. I'd have no wish to scatter my treasures too recklessly. Negro chants, dances of the houris? Is that what you want? Should I disappear or, plunging down to middle earth, seek out that Ring? What are you asking of me? I can conjure gold or cure your every malady. Just tell me.

Show some pride in me then. It is faith which calms, guides, cures. Come, one and all — even you, tiny child — let me console you, let all hearts swell for you — marvellous heart that it is!

Tragic labouring men! I ask for no prayers. Bolstered by your confidence,

I shall know happiness in this world.

Let us then spare a thought for me alone. I shall miss this world so little. O such luck, to be rid of suffering. My life was nothing but sweet foolishnesses, how regrettable it all was...

Bah! Let's pull terrible faces!

There's no doubt about it, we are beyond the reach of this world. Not a single sound. All tact has left me. Ah, my chateau, my Saxony, my elm wood! Evenings. mornings, nights, days... I am so weary!

Would that this hell of mine could serve as my anger, my conceit — and the hell of a caress into the bargain. Such a swelling concert of hells.

I am dying of lassitude. The tomb beckons, worms beckon, o horror of horrors. Satan, master of revelries, your charm would dissolve me. I bellow. I bellow. A single lunge of the devil's fork, a lash of flame.

Ah! To climb back towards life. Stare hard at all our deformities. And this poison too, this kiss one thousand times accursed. My weakness, the cruelties of this world. My God, for pity's sake hide me away. I esteem myself so little.

I am hidden — and I am not.

See how the fire is rising, engulfing the damned.

Deliriums

I
Foolish Virgin

Infernal Bridegroom

Listen in to the confessions of hell's companion...

O divine bridegroom, my Lord, do not set aside this confession by the saddest of your female servants. I am lost. I am drunk and disorderly. I am impure. What a life!

Pardon, divine Lord, pardon! Ah! Pardon! Such tears! And so many still to come, I hope.

Later, I shall know the divine bridegroom. I was born into his service. Let the evil one bruise and batter me now!

Here I am, in the world's cess pit. O my dearest friends...no, no longer my friends. Never have I known such torture...the beastliness of it all...

Ah! I am suffering. I cry out loud. Everything is granted me, burdened by the scorn of those most worthy of scorn...

Finally, let us repeat this confession out loud, saying it twenty times over — the sadder, the more beaten down it all sounds, the more insignificant.

I am a slave of the infernal bridegroom, he who made away with those foolish virgins. That is the demon I must contend with, neither spectre nor phantom. But I, who have mislaid all wisdom, who am damned and dead to the world — they will not kill me! How to describe it to you? My mouth is blocked. I am in mourning, I am tearful, I am afraid.

A little coolness please, Lord, I implore you, if it is your wish, if it is your wish to so grant it...

'I am a widow... I was a widow... oh yes, in former times I was a woman of the utmost seriousness, and I was not born to be a skeleton! He was barely a child. His mysterious delicacies had seduced me. I set aside all human duties to follow him. What a life! Real life is absent. We are not in this world. I go where he goes. I have to. And often he rises up against me, *me, poor soul that I am*. The Demon! He is a Demon, you know, not a man.

He says: 'I do not love womankind. Love exists to be re-invented, everyone knows that for a fact. They strive for comfort, assurance, it is all they are capable of. And, once secure, heart and beauty are set aside. There remains nothing but cold disdain, the tepid broth of marriage. Today. I see women about me, with their marks of happiness. We might have been friends once, torn to pieces by brutes with all the sensitivity of stacked wood...'

'I listen to him transforming infamy into glory, snatching charm from cruelty. "I hail from a distant race. My forefathers were Scandinavian, men who would guzzle the blood of their own thighs. Let me lacerate my entire body, tattoo myself all over, become as hideous as a Mongol. You will hear me bellowing through these streets. I want to be consumed by rage. Show me no jewels. Let me writhe and twist about on this carpet. My riches, let them be blood-spattered, everywhere. You'll never catch me working."

On certain nights, when his demon seized hold of me, we would roll around. I would be locked in mortal struggle with him. In those nights, often drunk, he would posture, in street or house, terrifying me unto death. 'Someone will slit your throat from side to side. It will be, as they say — let them quote me as saying this — "quite disgusting". Oh! Those days, when his sole wish was to strut up and down with the air of the practised criminal!

'Sometimes he speaks in a softened and soothing patois, of death calling out to repentance, of those genuinely unhappy ones beset by grievous labour, of departures which rend the heart. In those hovels where we wallowed in our drunken stupor, he would weep just to see those who surrounded us, all those miserable beasts. He raised up drunks from the black streets. He felt all the sadness of a wicked mother for little children gone astray. He flounced to the catechism with all the grace and the lightness of a tiny girl. He pretended to shed enlightenment everywhere — commerce, art, medicine. I followed him! Needs must!

'I saw with my own eyes all that conjured *mise-en-scène* — the clothes, the curtains, the furniture. I lent him arms to spar with, another face altogether. I saw everything that touched him, as he would have wished to create it for himself alone. When he fell into a curious inertia, I — yes, I — followed him, far, aping his actions strange and complicated, good or bad. I was convinced that I would never enter his world. In vigil beside his dear sleeping body, what hours of the night I watched over him, seeking out why he had such a wish to flee from reality. No man had taken such a vow.

I recognised — without fearing on his behalf — that he could be a serious danger to society. Is he perhaps harbouring life-changing secrets? No, he is merely looking, I told myself. He has all the charity of a sorcerer, and I am the prisoner of that charity.
No other soul would have strength — the strength of despair! — to bear it — to be protected and loved by him. Besides, I never imagined him with another soul: it was only his Angel, never the Angel of another. I truly believe I was nestled inside his soul as if in a palace emptied of all but you, who lacked nobility, that was all. Alas! I truly depended upon him. But what could he possibly want with an existence so cowardly and so tarnished? He would not make me better — unless perhaps he chose to kill me. Sadly, in sheer frustration, I would say to him: "I understand you." He shrugged his shoulders.

'In this way, with my sorrows ever self-renewing, and finding myself drifting ever further astray — in the eyes of all those who might have wished to anchor me, had I not been condemned and forgotten forever by everyone — I hungered more and more for his goodness. With his kisses and his suffocating embraces, it was a heaven, albeit a sombre one, through whose gates I was passing, and where I would have yearned to be left, poor, deaf, mute, blind. I had already grown so accustomed. I recognised us as two virtuous children, free to walk in this Paradise of sadness. We were in accord. Moved, we toiled together. But, after one particularly close embrace, he said: "how amusing all this will seem, when I am absent from you, this path along which you have walked. When you will no longer feel my arms across your neck, nor my heart to console you, nor the touch of my mouth on your eyes. Because it will be necessary for me to go away, far away, one day. There are others I must help: it is my duty. Although it will scarcely be to my taste... dearest soul." All of a sudden I could foresee it all, his departure, with myself in the grip of vertigo, plunged into a terrifying world of shadow: death itself. I made him promise not to leave go of me. He promised me twenty times over, the vow of a lover. It was as airily meaningless as if I had said: "I understand you."

'Ah! I have never been jealous of him. He will not abandon me, I believe that. What is to happen then? He knows no one. He will never work. His wish is to live the life of a somnambulist. Goodness and charity alone, would they give him any purchase in this world? For moments together, I forget this mood of pity into which I have fallen. He will make me strong. We will travel together. We will hunt in the deserts, sleep on the pavements of unknown cities, without cares or vexations. Or I awake, and all laws, all customs will have changed, thanks to his magical powers. This world, though remaining the same, will leave me here alone with my desires, my joys, my nonchalant ways. Oh, that life of adventure, so alive in the books of a child, will you grant it to me, I who have suffered so, by way of recompense? It is not possible. I am ignorant of his ideal. He has told me of his regrets, his hopes. It's no concern of mine, evidently. Does he speak to God? Perhaps I should appeal to god. I am sunken so deep into the abyss. I no longer know even how to pray.

'If he explained his sadnesses to me, would I understand them better than his mockery? He attacks me. He spends hours making me feel ashamed of everything which has been able to move my heart in this world. His indignation rises if I cry out.

'You see this elegant young man, how he enters into this house, so beautiful so calm. His name is Duval, Dufour, Armand, Maurice — how should I know? Some woman has pledged to love this badly behaved sot. She is dead now. She is a saint in heaven, for sure. You will bring about my death as he has brought about hers. It is our common fate, we, with such charitable hearts. Alas! There was a day when every man at large in this world seemed to him to be puppets in the grip of grotesque deliriums. His laughter, which went on and on, was frightful. Then he re-assumed the manners of a young mother, or of a beloved sister. If he were less savage, we would be saved! But his sweetness also hints of mortality. I have submitted to him. Ah! I am crazed!

'One day perhaps he will disappear, as if by some miracle, but I must know, if he is to return to the heavens. Let me witness with my own eyes, no matter how briefly, the assumption of my little sometime lover!'

Such a crazed household!

Deliriums

II
Alchemy of the Verb

All mine. This story of one of my bouts of insanity.

For so long now I have boasted of having every terrain possible within my grip, and I have found utterly ridiculous the pretensions of the painters and poets of this world of so called modernity.

Above all, I have loved Outsider Art, the art painted by idiots above doors; the daubed canvases of clowns; street tags: popular prints; outmoded literature; church latin; erotic books erratically spelled; the stories of our cobwebby forebears; fairy tales; children's books; old libretti; naïve rhymes; clunking rhythms.

I dreamt again of the crusades; voyages of discovery never before written about; republics unknown; wars of religion easily crushed; revolutions in manners; displacement of peoples, races, entire continents. I believed with a such a passion in all those species of enchantment.

I am the inventor of the colour of vowels — A black, E white, I red, O blue, U green. I put myself in charge of the form and the movement of each consonant, with my instinctive sense of rhythm. I flattered myself on having invented an entire poetic language, readily accessible, on this day or any other, to all the senses. I alone was its translator.

At first, in a blind fever of study, I wrote down my silences, my nights, minutely noting the inexpressible. I held every vertigo steady as a rock.

―――

      Far from birds, flocks, and all these village people,
      what was I dreaming, on my knees
      there in that heathland,
      encompassed by such
      tender hazel trees,
      in that fog of afternoon's fashioning,
      warmish and green....

Tell me what I might drink
from the Oise, that youthful river,
beneath those voiceless elms,
on that flowerless earth, sky darkened?
Should I sip from those yellow gourds,
far from home, my darling?

I fashioned for myself
my own scruffy inn sign.
A storm blew up just then,
chasing the clouds.
In the evening.
water streaming down from the woods
disappeared into virgin sands.
Crying out, I saw gold ahead —
and could not drink it.

———

At four in the morning,
at summer's height,
beneath tree shade,
the smell of festive evenings
fades and fades and fades...

Beyond, in their great shipyard,
beneath the blazing sun of the Hesperides,
they are already busy —
stripped to their shirt sleeves —
the mighty Carpenters.

Far across those mossy Deserts,
in such unheard of tranquillity,
they are preparing the precious canvases
on which the entire town
will daub its phantom skies.

All hail to the workers,
charmed subjects of
some Babylonian king.

Venus! Be banished from these lovers
whose souls even now
are being crowned...

O queen of shepherds,
bear your brandy to the workers,
let all their strength be at peace
as they bathe in the mid-day sea.

The old ways of poetry played their part in my alchemy of the verb.

I accustomed myself to hallucination pure and simple: clear as day is day, I saw a mosque where a factory had once been; a drummers' school created by angels; carriages on the roads to heaven; a salon at the bottom of the lake; monsters, mysteries; vaudeville showed off its marvels in front of me.

Then I explained my magical sophistries by the hallucinatory power of words.

I finished by calling the disorder of my spirit a sacred thing. I was idleness itself, in the grip of a dragging fever. I envied the happiness of beasts; caterpillars and their innocence of limb; moles; the very sleep of virginity.

My character sharpened. I bade goodbye to the world with balladry:

Song of the Highest Tower

Oh let it come, let it come,
that time for which we yearn.

I have shown such patience,
to the point of forgetfulness.
Fears and sufferings
have ascended to the heavens,
and this evil thirst
is darkening my veins.

Oh let it come, let it come,
that time for which we yearn.

To such forgetfulness
is this land abandoned,
swollen and flowering
with incense and tares,
and all around us — listen! —
the frantic buzzing
of filthy flies.

Oh let it come, let it come,
that time for which we yearn.

I loved the desert, the burnt out orchards, the shops in their fading, the drinks barely warm. I dragged myself through the stinking streets, and, with eyes closed, offered myself up to the sun, that god of fire.

'General, if there yet remains a single ancient cannon on your ruined ramparts, bombard us with your lumps of dried earth. Up to the very windows of their splendid shops! Into the salons! Cause this very town to eat its own dust. Oxidise these gargoyles. Fill up the boudoirs with your powder of burning rubies...'

Oh! See how the drunken fly blunders around the inn's urinal, besotted by borage, reduced to nothingness by a sunbeam.

Hunger

If any taste remains to me,
let it be for this earth and these stones.
I breakfast, always, on air,
rock, iron, coal...

Turn, hungers. Graze, hungers
on this meadow of sonorities.
Pluck the sweet venom
from the convolvulus.

Eat these crushed pebbles,
ancient stones of churches,
gravel beds of inundations,
breads flung across grey valleys.

The wolf howled beneath the leaves
spitting out gorgeous feathers
from his meal of game.
Like him, I consume myself wholly.

Salads, fruits
await only their gathering,
but the spider in the hedge
eats nothing but violets.

Let me sleep! Let me boil
on the altars of Solomon.
The broth streams down through the rust
and mingles with the Kedron.

Finally, o happiness, o reason, I stole from the sky the darkness of its azure, and I came alive, golden spark of nature's light. For sheer joy, I assumed an expression as doltish and and bewildered as possible.

Found once again!
What? Eternity!
Sea once more
at one with the sun.

Eternal soul,
cling to your vows
for all night's aloneness
and the day on fire...

You separate yourself
from all human suffering.
Such common raptures!
You soar — but whither...

All hope abandoned
no more rising
all science, all patience
punishment is certain

No more tomorrow
embers of satin
let duty be manifest
in your ardour.

Found once again!
What? Eternity!
Sea once more
at one with the sun.

I transformed myself into a fabulous operatic production. I was sure that everything on this earth would suffer the fatality of happiness — to be active is not to live, it is to squander one's strength in a terrible nervelessness. Morality means pulping the brain.

To each and every being, several other lives seemed owed to me. This man has no clue what he is up to: he is an angel. That family is a pack of ravening dogs. In front of several men, I chatted noisily, at the moment which belonged to one of their other lives. In this way, I have grown enamoured of a pig.

None of the misconstructions of madness — that madness trapped within — have been forgotten by me. I could repeat them all over again. I know how the system works, matey.

My health was under threat. Terror had me in its grip. I fell into a sleep which lasted for several days on end and, once stirred, I continued with all those sad dreams. I was braced for death, and by a road filled with dangers my weakness dragged me to the very edge of the world, to those Cimmerian lands, homeland of the shadow and the typhoon.

I had to travel, as a distraction from that swarm of enchantments settled in my brain. Across the sea, which I loved for its ability to cleanse me of all stains. I saw the cross rise up — such a consolation! I had been damned by the rainbow. Happiness was my fatal wound, my remorse, my worm in the bud: my life would always be too overwhelming for any devotion to strength and beauty.

Happiness! Its tooth, sweet unto death, warned me of the cock's crowing at the daylight hour, when Christ comes, in the most sombre of towns...

> O seasons, o chateaux!
> What soul is without stain?
>
> I have pursued the magic of happiness,
> which must all consume.
>
> I greet it, each time
> the Gallic cock crows.
>
> Ah! To wish no more....
> It has seized hold of my life.
>
> This charm has taken body and soul captive,
> and nullified all my efforts.
>
> O seasons, oh chateaux!
>
> The hour that it flees, alas,
> will be the hour of my death.

Let past be past. Today, I know what it is to greet beauty!

The Impossible

Ah! That childhood life of mine, taking the high road in all weathers, sober as a god, more disinterested than the finest of beggars, proud to own no country, no friends — what stupidity all that was! And to be aware of it only now!

Am I not right to pour scorn on Mr Average, the one who always squeezes you in a bear hug, who preys on the cleanness, the good health of women, today of all days, when they have drifted so far away from us...

I'm right to show such disdain.

I'm doing a bunk.

I'm escaping.

And here's what it's all about...

Yesterday I sighed to myself all over again. Heavens above! Aren't there enough damned souls down here? I've wasted enough time already with that lot! I know them all, through and through. We recognise each other, always; we wallow in our mutual disgust. Charity! Unknown to us. Yet we're polite enough. Our relations with the world suit us well enough. Is that surprising?

The world! All those wheeler-dealers in naivety! We are not dishonoured. But how would the chosen ones receive us? There are the spiteful, the brimming-with-joy. They are the falsely chosen ones through and through. We need such gall, such humility just to confront them. And yet are they not the only chosen ones? Don't expect a blessing!

Having re-discovered two a'porth of good sense... It will go again soon enough. I can see that all this malaise is due to not having worked out soon enough that we are in — and of — the West! Those Western boglands!

Not that the light has changed, the form of things weakened, movement gone astray. Good! Let my spirit take on the burden of all the cruelties we have suffered since the East bade its fond farewell to us. My spirit yearns for it still!

My two a'porth of good sense, all fled! Spirit seizes hold of the wheel. It wants me to be in the West. I'd have to shut it up to do as I pleased.

Let the devil take the palms of the martyrs, all the splendours of art, the pride of inventors, the yearnings of the pillagers. I went back to the East and to wisdom, its eternal source. It seems now that it was nothing but a dream of grotesque idleness!

Nevertheless, I barely dreamt of the sufferings of modernity. The bastard wisdom of the Koran had never been in my sights.

But is there not real torture in the declarations of that so called science of Christianity? Man juggles with these things, sifting all the evidence, swelling with pride as he repeats the same truths over, knowing no other life... Torture so subtle, so naïve, source of all my spiritual wanderings. Enough to make nature yawn perhaps. M.Prudhomme and Christ our Lord, co-evals...

Is it not because we cultivate the fog! We masticate our fevers with watery vegetables. And drunkenness! And tobacco! And our worship at the altar of ignorance! Is not all that some way off real thinking, the wisdom of the Orient, that primitive fatherland? Why the need of a modern world at all, if we can conjure such poisons?

Those of the church will say: that's understood. But it's of Eden that you want to speak. There's nothing for you in all that history of the Orientals — That's true enough. I was indeed thinking of Eden! What's with all this dreaming of the purity of ancient races! Am I nuts?

The philosophers: the world is ageless. Humanity shifts about, it's as simple as that. You are in the West, but you are also free to live in your East, no matter how antique it needs to be — and to live there in prosperity. Don't be amongst the defeated. Philosophers, you belong to the West.

Beware, spirit of mine. Don't opt for the violence of salvation. Do your pull ups! Science never travels fleet enough for the likes of us!

But even I can see that my spirit is nodding.

If it was really awake, always, and from this moment on, we'd soon arrive at the truth, which may even be encircling us with its weeping angels! If it had been jerked awake at this very moment, I would have succumbed to such deleterious instincts, in an epoch as immemorial as this one. If it had always been wide awake, I'd be drifting along in a boat crammed to the gills with all wisdom's bullion.

O purity! Purity!

At this moment of wakefulness, I have been gifted with this vision of purity! By the spirit one rises to God!

Oh wretched misfortune!

Lightning

Human toil! That terrible explosion which lights up my abyss from time to time.

'Nothing is vanity; forever onward with science' shouts the Ecclesiastes of our day, that is to say *everyone*. Meanwhile, the corpses of merchants and do-nothings fall across the heart of all those others.

Ah! Quickly, fairly quickly; over there, on the far side of the night, the eternal recompenses of the future. Can we escape them?

What am I capable of? I know work to the bone; and science is just too slow... Let my prayers gallop away, and the light grumble and growl at me. I can see it so well. It's too simple and too warm; they will do without me. I have my duties to attend to. I shall be proud as others are proud when I set them aside.

My life is exhausted. Let's go then; let's pretend, slop around, o pity! And we will survive only to amuse ourselves, dreaming of lovers, monsters and universes of pure fantasy, in which we, drowsy with self-pity, quarrel with the appearances of the world, clown, beggar, artist, bandit – and even preacher! On my hospital bed, the reek of incense, so powerful, has come back to me; guardian of the sacred aromas, confessor, martyr...

I recognise it there, my filthy childhood education. Then what! My twentieth year approaches, if the others also agree to be twenty...

No! No! At this moment I have taken up arms against death! Work is too light for one so conceited: my betrayal in the world's eyes would be all too brief a torture. At the last moment, I would lunge to the right, to the left...

Well then – oh! poor, cherished soul, would eternity not be lost for us!

Morning

Is it not true that I once had a pleasing childhood, heroic, fabulous, of the kind to be written down on leaves of gold — too much good luck!

By what curse or error have I deserved such weakness? You who proclaim that even beasts can sob with regret, that the ill lose all hope, that the dead dream so badly, try to speak to me of my fall and of my sleep. I can no longer explain to myself how the beggar mutters his *Paters* and his *Ave Marias* continuously... *I no longer have the gift of speech!*

Today, however, I believe that my pact with hell has finished. It was ok, hell; it was hell without a doubt, the old hell, whose gates the son of man flung back.

From the same desert, on the same night, my tired eyes always wake to silver starlight, always, although the Kings of life, the three mages, the heart, the soul, the spirit, are not distracted. When shall we go beyond the shorelines and the mountains, to greet the birth of new work, new wisdom, the flight of tyrants and demons, the end of all superstition, to adore — we, the first! — Christmas on this earth!

The song of the heavens, the march of people! Slaves, let us not curse life.

Adieu

Autumn already! But why regret the loss of an eternal sun if we are committed to the discovery of light divine — far from those who die by the season.

Autumn. Our little boat, risen up through the still fog, turns its prow towards the port of misery, the enormous citadel with its sky tainted by fire and mud. Ah! Those rotten rags, bread soaked in rain water, the thousand loves which have crucified me! Can she never stop, this ghoulish queen of millions of souls and bodies dead *and which shall* be *judged.* I see myself again, skin scarred by mud and pestilence, hair and armpits wormy, with yet grosser worms eating at my heart, stretched out amongst ageless strangers, feelingless. I might have died there!

Frightful memories! How I despise poverty.

And I fear winter oncoming because it is the season of comfort!

From time to time, I see in the sky this vision of endless beaches covered by joyous white nations. Above me, a mighty vessel of gold flourishes its multi-coloured flags in the breezes of morning. I have created all these festivals, all the triumphs, all the dramas. I have tried to invent new flowers, new flesh, new tongues. I have believed myself to be in possession of supernatural powers. Oh well! I must bury my imagination and my memories. Snatch him away, this artist and teller of tales, glorious and beautiful.

I! I who have called myself mage or angel, having shrugged off all morality, am back now, earth-grounded, with a solemn duty to seek out, and all reality's roughness to embrace! Peasant!

Am I mistaken? Would charity be the sister of death, for me? Finally, I will beg pardon for having fed myself on lies. Let's be off then.

But not a single hand in friendship? And where to run to for help?

Yes, this is the new hour at the very least, in its extreme severity.
For I could say that the victory is mine: the grinding of teeth, the hiss of

flame, even the stench of your breathed sighs, it is all falling away. All the disgusting memories are fading away. My final regrets, let me roll them out: jealousy for all the beggars, the brigands, companions of death, all those who must trail along behind.

All damned, if I avenged myself!

It is necessary to be completely modern.

No canticles: your step must hold firm. Hard night! The dried blood is smoking across my face, and I have nothing behind me, nothing but this horrible shrub! Spiritual battle is as tough and as brutal as combat between men; but the vision of justice is God's pleasure alone.

Meanwhile, we teeter on the brink. Let us breathe in all this vigour, all this genuine tenderness. And as dawn breaks, armed with all the ardour of our patience, we shall enter into the magnificent towns.

What was I just saying about the hand of friendship? One great advantage is that I can laugh about all those lies of old loves, and smite with the rod of shame those deceiving couples. I have seen the hell of women over there, and now I shall have the leisure to embrace the truth in a single soul, a single body.

August–October 2019

Enfin, je demanderai pardon pour m'être nourri de mensonge. Et allons.

Mais pas une main amie! et où puiser le secours?

Oui, l'heure nouvelle est au moins très sévère.

Car je puis dire que la victoire m'est acquise: les grincements de dents, les sifflements de feu, les soupirs empestés se modèrent. Tous les souvenirs immondes s'effacent. Mes derniers regrets détalent, — des jalousies pour les mendiants, les brigands, les amis de la mort, les arriérés de toutes sortes. — Damnés, si je me vengeais!

Il faut être absolument moderne.

Point de cantiques: tenir le pas gagné. Dure nuit! le sang séché fume sur ma face, et je n'ai rien derrière moi, que cet horrible arbrisseau!... Le combat spirituel est aussi brutal que la bataille d'hommes; mais la vision de la justice est le plaisir de Dieu seul.

Cependant c'est la veille. Recevons tous les influx de vigueur et de tendresse réelle. Et à l'aurore, armés d'une ardente patience, nous entrerons aux splendides villes.

Que parlais-je de main amie! un bel avantage, c'est que je puis rire des vieilles amours mensongères, et frapper de honte ces couples menteurs, — j'ai vu l'enfer des femmes là-bas; — et il me sera loisible de posséder la vérité dans une âme et un corps.

Avril-août, 1873.

Adieu

L'automne déjà! — Mais pourquoi regretter un éternel soleil, si nous sommes engagés à la découverte de la clarté divine, — loin des gens qui meurent sur les saisons.

L'automne. Notre barque élevée dans les brumes immobiles tourne vers le port de la misère, la cité énorme au ciel taché de feu et de boue. Ah! les haillons pourris, le pain trempé de pluie, l'ivresse, les mille amours qui m'ont crucifié! Elle ne finira donc point cette goule reine de millions d'âmes et de corps morts et qui seront jugés! Je me revois la peau rongée par la boue et la peste, des vers plein les cheveux et les aisselles et encore de plus gros vers dans le cœur, étendu parmi les inconnus sans âge, sans sentiment... J'aurais pu y mourir... L'affreuse évocation! J'exècre la misère.

Et je redoute l'hiver parce que c'est la saison du comfort!

Quelquefois je vois au ciel des plages sans fin couvertes de blanches nations en joie. Un grand vaisseau d'or, au-dessus de moi, agite ses pavillons multicolores sous les brises du matin. J'ai créé toutes les fêtes, tous les triomphes, tous les drames. J'ai essayé d'inventer de nouvelles fleurs, de nouveaux astres, de nouvelles chairs, de nouvelles langues. J'ai cru acquérir des pouvoirs surnaturels. Eh bien! je dois enterrer mon imagination et mes souvenirs! Une belle gloire d'artiste et de conteur emportée!

Moi! moi qui me suis dit mage ou ange, dispensé de toute morale, je suis rendu au sol, avec un devoir à chercher, et la réalité rugueuse à étreindre! Paysan!

Suis-je trompé, la charité serait-elle sœur de la mort, pour moi?

Matin

N'eus-je pas une fois une jeunesse aimable, héroïque, fabuleuse, à écrire sur des feuilles d'or, — trop de chance! Par quel crime, par quelle erreur, ai-je mérité ma faiblesse actuelle? Vous qui prétendez que des bêtes poussent des sanglots de chagrin, que des malades désespèrent, que des morts rêvent mal, tâchez de raconter ma chute et mon sommeil. Moi, je ne puis pas plus m'expliquer que le mendiant avec ses continuels Pater et Ave Maria. Je ne sais plus parler!

Pourtant, aujourd'hui, je crois avoir fini la relation de mon enfer. C'était bien l'enfer; l'ancien, celui dont le fils de l'homme ouvrit les portes.

Du même désert, à la même nuit, toujours mes yeux las se réveillent à l'étoile d'argent, toujours, sans que s'émeuvent les Rois de la vie, les trois mages, le cœur, l'âme, l'esprit. Quand irons-nous, par-delà les grèves et les monts, saluer la naissance du travail nouveau, la sagesse nouvelle, la fuite des tyrans et des démons, la fin de la superstition, adorer — les premiers! — Noël sur la terre!

Le chant des cieux, la marche des peuples! Esclaves ne maudissons pas la vie.

L'Éclair

Le travail humain! c'est l'explosion qui éclaire mon abîme de temps en temps.

"Rien n'est vanité; à la science, et en avant!" crie l'Ecclésiaste moderne, c'est-à-dire Tout le monde. Et pourtant les cadavres des méchants et des fainéants tombent sur le cœur des autres... Ah! vite, vite un peu; là-bas, par-delà la nuit, ces récompenses futures, éternelles... les échappons-nous?...

— Qu'y puis-je? Je connais le travail; et la science est trop lente. Que la prière galope et que la lumière gronde... je le vois bien. C'est trop simple, et il fait trop chaud; on se passera de moi. J'ai mon devoir, j'en serai fier à la façon de plusieurs, en le mettant de côté.

Ma vie est usée. Allons! feignons, fainéantons, ô pitié! Et nous existerons en nous amusant, en rêvant amours monstres et univers fantastiques, en nous plaignant et en querellant les apparences du monde, saltimbanque, mendiant, artiste, bandit, — prêtre! Sur mon lit d'hôpital, l'odeur de l'encens m'est revenue si puissante; gardien des aromates sacrés, confesseur, martyr...

Je reconnais là ma sale éducation d'enfance. Puis quoi!... Aller mes vingt ans, si les autres vont vingt ans...

Non! non! à présent je me révolte contre la mort! Le travail paraît trop léger à mon orgueil: ma trahison au monde serait un supplice trop court. Au dernier moment, j'attaquerais à droite, à gauche...

Alors, — oh! — chère pauvre âme, l'éternité serait-elle pas perdue pour nous!

Les philosophes: le monde n'a pas d'âge. L'humanité se déplace, simplement. Vous êtes en Occident, mais libre d'habiter dans votre Orient, quelque ancien qu'il vous le faille, — et d'y habiter bien. Ne soyez pas un vaincu. Philosophes, vous êtes de votre Occident.

Mon esprit, prends garde. Pas de partis de salut violents. Exerce-toi! — Ah! la science ne va pas assez vite pour nous!

Mais je m'aperçois que mon esprit dort.

S'il était éveillé toujours à partir de ce moment, nous serions bientôt à la vérité, qui peut-être nous entoure avec ses anges pleurant!... — S'il avait été éveillé jusqu'à ce moment-ci, c'est que je n'aurais pas cédé aux instincts délétères, à une époque immémoriale!... — S'il avait toujours été bien éveillé, je voguerais en pleine sagesse!...

Ô pureté! pureté!

C'est cette minute d'éveil qui m'a donné la vision de la pureté! — Par l'esprit on va à Dieu!

Déchirante infortune!

absolument se charger de tous les développements cruels qu'a subis l'esprit depuis la fin de l'Orient... Il en veut, mon esprit!

Mes deux sous de raison sont finis! — L'esprit est autorité, il veut que je sois en Occident. Il faudrait le faire taire pour conclure comme je voulais.

J'envoyais au diable les palmes des martyrs, les rayons de l'art, l'orgueil des inventeurs, l'ardeur des pillards; je retournais à l'Orient et à la sagesse première et éternelle. — Il paraît que c'est un rêve de paresse grossière!

Pourtant, je ne songeais guère au plaisir d'échapper aux souffrances modernes. Je n'avais pas en vue la sagesse bâtarde du Coran. — Mais n'y a-t-il pas un supplice réel en ce que, depuis cette déclaration de la science, le christianisme, l'homme se joue, se prouve les évidences, se gonfle du plaisir de répéter ces preuves, et ne vit que comme cela! Torture subtile, niaise; source de mes divagations spirituelles. La nature pourrait s'ennuyer, peut-être! M. Prudhomme est né avec le Christ.

N'est-ce pas parce que nous cultivons la brume! Nous mangeons la fièvre avec nos légumes aqueux. Et l'ivrognerie! et le tabac! et l'ignorance! et les dévouements! — Tout cela est-il assez loin de la pensée de la sagesse de l'Orient, la patrie primitive? Pourquoi un monde moderne, si de pareils poisons s'inventent!

Les gens d'Église diront: C'est compris. Mais vous voulez parler de l'Eden. Rien pour vous dans l'histoire des peuples orientaux. — C'est vrai; c'est à l'Eden que je songeais! Qu'est-ce que c'est pour mon rêve, cette pureté des races antiques!

L'impossible

Ah! cette vie de mon enfance, la grande route par tous les temps, sobre surnaturellement, plus désintéressé que le meilleur des mendiants, fier de n'avoir ni pays, ni amis, quelle sottise c'était. — Et je m'en aperçois seulement!

— J'ai eu raison de mépriser ces bonshommes qui ne perdraient pas l'occasion d'une caresse, parasites de la propreté et de la santé de nos femmes, aujourd'hui qu'elles sont si peu d'accord avec nous.

J'ai eu raison dans tous mes dédains: puisque je m'évade!

Je m'évade!

Je m'explique.

Hier encore, je soupirais: "Ciel! sommes-nous assez de damnés ici-bas! Moi j'ai tant de temps déjà dans leur troupe! Je les connais tous. Nous nous reconnaissons toujours; nous nous dégoûtons. La charité nous est inconnue. Mais nous sommes polis; nos relations avec le monde sont très convenables." Est-ce étonnant? Le monde! les marchands, les naïfs! — Nous ne sommes pas déshonorés. — Mais les élus, comment nous recevraient-ils? Or il y a des gens hargneux et joyeux, de faux élus, puisqu'il nous faut de l'audace ou de l'humilité pour les aborder. Ce sont les seuls élus. Ce ne sont pas des bénisseurs!

M'étant retrouvé deux sous de raison — ça passe vite! — je vois que mes malaises viennent de ne m'être pas figuré assez tôt que nous sommes à l'Occident. Les marais occidentaux! Non que je croie la lumière altérée, la forme exténuée, le mouvement égaré... Bon! voici que mon esprit veut

Ô saisons, ô châteaux!
Quelle âme est sans défauts?

J'ai fait la magique étude
Du bonheur, qu'aucun n'élude.

Salut à lui, chaque fois
Que chante le coq gaulois.

Ah! je n'aurai plus d'envie:
Il s'est chargé de ma vie.

Ce charme a pris âme et corps
Et dispersé les efforts.

Ô saisons, ô châteaux!

L'heure de sa fuite, hélas!
Sera l'heure du trépas.

Ô saisons, ô châteaux!

———

Cela s'est passé. Je sais aujourd'hui saluer la beauté.

Je devins un opéra fabuleux: je vis que tous les êtres ont une fatalité de bonheur: l'action n'est pas la vie, mais une façon de gâcher quelque force, un énervement. La morale est la faiblesse de la cervelle.

À chaque être, plusieurs autres vies mes semblaient dues. Ce monsieur ne sait ce qu'il fait: il est un ange. Cette famille est une nichée de chiens. Devant plusieurs hommes, je causai tout haut avec un moment d'une de leurs autres vies. — Ainsi, j'ai aimé un porc.

Aucun des sophismes de la folie, — la folie qu'on enferme, — n'a été oublié par moi: je pourrais les redire tous, je tiens le système.

Ma santé fut menacée. La terreur venait. Je tombais dans des sommeils de plusieurs jours, et, levé, je continuais les rêves les plus tristes. J'étais mûr pour le trépas, et par une route de dangers ma faiblesse me menait aux confins du monde et de la Cimmérie, patrie de l'ombre et des tourbillons.

Je dus voyager, distraire les enchantements assemblés sur mon cerveau. Sur la mer, que j'aimais comme si elle eût dû me laver d'une souillure, je voyais se lever la croix consolatrice. J'avais été damné par l'arc-en-ciel. Le Bonheur était ma fatalité, mon remords, mon ver: ma vie serait toujours trop immense pour être dévouée à la force et à la beauté.

Le Bonheur! Sa dent, douce à la mort, m'avertissait au chant du coq, — ad matutinum, au Christus venit, — dans les plus sombres villes:

Enfin, ô bonheur, ô raison, j'écartai du ciel l'azur, qui est du noir, et je vécus, étincelle d'or de la lumière nature. De joie, je prenais une expression bouffonne et égarée au possible:

Elle est retrouvée!
Quoi? l'éternité.
C'est la mer mêlée
   Au soleil.

Mon âme éternelle,
Observe ton vœu
Malgré la nuit seule
Et le jour en feu.

Donc tu te dégages
Des humains suffrages,
Des communs élans!
Tu voles selon...

— Jamais l'espérance.
Pas d'orietur.
Science et patience,
Le supplice est sûr.

Plus de lendemain,
Braises de satin,
Votre ardeur
Est le devoir.

Elle est retrouvée!
— Quoi? — l'Éternité.
C'est la mer mêlée
   Au soleil.

FAIM

Si j'ai du goût, ce n'est guère
Que pour la terre et les pierres.
Je déjeune toujours d'air,
De roc, de charbons, de fer.

Mes faims, tournez. Paissez, faims,
 Le pré des sons.
Attirez le gai venin
Des liserons.

Mangez les cailloux qu'on brise,
Les vieilles pierres d'églises;
Les galets des vieux déluges,
Pains semés dans les vallées grises.

———

Le loup criait sous les feuilles
En crachant les belles plumes
De son repas de volailles:
Comme lui je me consume.

Les salades, les fruits
N'attendent que la cueillette;
Mais l'araignée de la haie
Ne mange que des violettes.

Que je dorme! que je bouille
Aux autels de Salomon.
Le bouillon court sur la rouille,
Et se mêle au Cédron.

J'ai tant fait patience
Qu'à jamais j'oublie.
Craintes et souffrances
Aux cieux sont parties.
Et la soif malsaine
Obscurcit mes veines.

Qu'il vienne, qu'il vienne,
Le temps dont on s'éprenne.

Telle la prairie
À l'oubli livrée,
Grandie, et fleurie
D'encens et d'ivraies,
Au bourdon farouche
Des sales mouches.

Qu'il vienne, qu'il vienne,
Le temps dont on s'éprenne.

J'aimai le désert, les vergers brûlés, les boutiques fanées, les boissons tiédies. Je me traînais dans les ruelles puantes et, les yeux fermés, je m'offrais au soleil, dieu de feu.

"Général, s'il reste un vieux canon sur tes remparts en ruines, bombarde-nous avec des blocs de terre sèche. Aux glaces des magasins splendides! dans les salons! Fais manger sa poussière à la ville. Oxyde les gargouilles. Emplis les boudoirs de poudre de rubis brûlante..."

Oh! le moucheron enivré à la pissotière de l'auberge, amoureux de la bourrache, et que dissout un rayon!

Ô, pour ces Ouvriers charmants
Sujets d'un roi de Babylone,
Vénus! quitte un instant les Amants
Dont l'âme est en couronne.

Ô Reine des Bergers,
Porte aux travailleurs l'eau-de-vie,
Que leurs forces soient en paix
En attendant le bain dans la mer à midi.

―――――――

La vieillerie poétique avait une bonne part dans mon alchimie du verbe.

Je m'habituai à l'hallucination simple: je voyais très franchement une mosquée à la place d'une usine, une école de tambours faite par des anges, des calèches sur les routes du ciel, un salon au fond d'un lac; les monstres, les mystères; un titre de vaudeville dressait des épouvantes devant moi.

Puis j'expliquai mes sophismes magiques avec l'hallucination des mots!

Je finis par trouver sacré le désordre de mon esprit. J'étais oisif, en proie à une lourde fièvre: j'enviais la félicité des bêtes, — les chenilles, qui représentent l'innocence des limbes, les taupes, le sommeil de la virginité!

Mon caractère s'aigrissait. Je disais adieu au monde dans d'espèces de romances:

CHANSON DE LA PLUS HAUTE TOUR

Qu'il vienne, qu'il vienne,
Le temps dont on s'éprenne.

Entourée de tendres bois de noisetiers,
Dans un brouillard d'après-midi tiède et vert?

Que pouvais-je boire dans cette jeune Oise,
— Ormeaux sans voix, gazon sans fleurs, ciel couvert!
Boire à ces gourdes jaunes, loin de ma case
Chérie? Quelque liqueur d'or qui fait suer.

Je faisais une louche enseigne d'auberge.
— Un orage vint chasser le ciel. Au soir
L'eau des bois se perdait sur les sables vierges,
Le vent de Dieu jetait des glaçons aux mares;

Pleurant, je voyais de l'or — et ne pus boire. —

À quatre heures du matin, l'été,
Le sommeil d'amour dure encore.
Sous les bocages s'évapore
L'odeur du soir fêté.

Là-bas, dans leur vaste chantier
Au soleil des Hespérides,
Déjà s'agitent — en bras de chemise —
Les Charpentiers.

Dans leurs Déserts de mousse, tranquilles,
Ils préparent les lambris précieux
Où la ville
Peindra de faux cieux.

DÉLIRES

II

Alchimie du verbe

À moi. L'histoire d'une de mes folies.

Depuis longtemps je me vantais de posséder tous les paysages possibles, et trouvais dérisoire les célébrités de la peinture et de la poésie moderne.

J'aimais les peintures idiotes, dessus de portes, décors, toiles de saltimbanques, enseignes, enluminures populaires; la littérature démodée, latin d'église, livres érotiques sans orthographe, romans de nos aïeules, contes de fées, petits livres de l'enfance, opéras vieux, refrains niais, rythmes naïfs.

Je rêvais croisades, voyages de découvertes dont on n'a pas de relations, républiques sans histoires, guerres de religion étouffées, révolutions de mœurs, déplacements de races et de continents: je croyais à tous les enchantements.

J'inventai la couleur des voyelles! — A noir, E blanc, I rouge, O bleu, U vert. — Je réglai la forme et le mouvement de chaque consonne, et, avec des rythmes instinctifs, je me flattai d'inventer un verbe poétique accessible, un jour ou l'autre, à tous les sens. Je réservais la traduction.

Ce fut d'abord une étude. J'écrivais des silences, des nuits, je notais l'inexprimable. Je fixais des vertiges.

Loin des oiseaux, des troupeaux, des villageoises,
Que buvais-je, à genoux dans cette bruyère

restant le même, me laissera à mes désirs, joies, nonchalances. Oh! la vie d'aventures qui existe dans les livres des enfants, pour me récompenser, j'ai tant souffert, me la donneras-tu? Il ne peut pas. J'ignore son idéal. Il m'a dit avoir des regrets, des espoirs: cela ne doit pas me regarder. Parle-t-il à Dieu? Peut-être devrais-je m'adresser à Dieu. Je suis au plus profond de l'abîme, et je ne sais plus prier.

"S'il m'expliquait ses tristesses, les comprendrais-je plus que ses railleries? Il m'attaque, il passe des heures à me faire honte de tout ce qui m'a pu toucher au monde, et s'indigne si je pleure.

"Tu vois cet élégant jeune homme, entrant dans la belle et calme maison: il s'appelle Duval, Dufour, Armand, Maurice, que sais-je? Une femme s'est dévouée à aimer ce méchant idiot: elle est morte, c'est certes une sainte au ciel, à présent. Tu me feras mourir comme il a fait mourir cette femme. C'est notre sort, à nous, cœurs charitables..." Hélas! il avait des jours où tous les hommes agissant lui paraissaient les jouets de délires grotesques: il riait affreusement, longtemps. — Puis, il reprenait ses manières de jeune mère, de sœur aimée. S'il était moins sauvage, nous serions sauvés! Mais sa douceur aussi est mortelle. Je lui suis soumise. — Ah! je suis folle!

"Un jour peut-être il disparaîtra merveilleusement; mais il faut que je sache, s'il doit remonter à un ciel, que je voie un peu l'assomption de mon petit ami!"

Drôle de ménage!

s'il ne me faisait pas mourir! Tristement dépitée, je lui dis quelquefois: "Je te comprends." Il haussait les épaules.

"Ainsi, mon chagrin se renouvelant sans cesse, et me trouvant plus égarée à mes yeux, — comme à tous les yeux qui auraient voulu me fixer, si je n'eusse été condamnée pour jamais à l'oubli de tous! — j'avais de plus en plus faim de sa bonté. Avec ses baisers et ses étreintes amies, c'était bien un ciel, un sombre ciel, où j'entrais, et où j'aurais voulu être laissée, pauvre, sourde, muette, aveugle. Déjà j'en prenais l'habitude. Je nous voyais comme deux bons enfants, libres de se promener dans le Paradis de tristesse. Nous nous accordions. Bien émus, nous travaillions ensemble. Mais, après une pénétrante caresse, il disait: "Comme ça te paraîtra drôle, quand je n'y serai plus, ce par quoi tu as passé. Quand tu n'auras plus mes bras sous ton cou, ni mon cœur pour t'y reposer, ni cette bouche sur tes yeux. Parce qu'il faudra que je m'en aille, très loin, un jour. Puis il faut que j'en aide d'autres: c'est mon devoir. Quoique ce ne soit guère ragoûtant..., chère âme..." Tout de suite je me pressentais, lui parti, en proie au vertige, précipitée dans l'ombre la plus affreuse: la mort. Je lui faisais promettre qu'il ne me lâcherait pas. Il l'a faite vingt fois, cette promesse d'amant. C'était aussi frivole que moi lui disant: "Je te comprends."

"Ah! je n'ai jamais été jalouse de lui. Il ne me quittera pas, je crois. Que devenir? Il n'a pas une connaissance; il ne travaillera jamais. Il veut vivre somnambule. Seules, sa bonté et sa charité lui donneraient-elles droit dans le monde réel? Par instants, j'oublie la pitié où je suis tombée: lui me rendra forte, nous voyagerons, nous chasserons dans les déserts, nous dormirons sur les pavés des villes inconnues, sans soins, sans peines. Ou je me réveillerai, et les lois et les mœurs auront changé, — grâce à son pouvoir magique, — le monde, en

"Parfois il parle, en une façon de patois attendri, de la mort qui fait repentir, des malheureux qui existent certainement, des travaux pénibles, des départs qui déchirent les cœurs. Dans les bouges où nous enivrions, il pleurait en considérant ceux qui nous entouraient, bétail de la misère. Il relevait les ivrognes dans les rues noires. Il avait la pitié d'une mère méchante pour les petits enfants. — Il s'en allait avec des gentillesses de petite fille au catéchisme. — Il feignait d'être éclairé sur tout, commerce, art, médecine. — Je le suivais, il le faut!

"Je voyais tout le décor dont, en esprit, il s'entourait; vêtements, draps, meubles: je lui prêtais des armes, une autre figure. Je voyais tout ce qui le touchait, comme il aurait voulu le créer pour lui. Quand il me semblait avoir l'esprit inerte, je le suivais, moi, dans des actions étranges et compliquées, loin, bonnes ou mauvaises: j'étais sûre de ne jamais entrer dans son monde. A côté de son cher corps endormi, que d'heures des nuits j'ai veillé, cherchant pourquoi il voulait tant s'évader de la réalité. Jamais l'homme n'eut pareil vœu. Je reconnaissais, — sans craindre pour lui, — qu'il pouvait être un sérieux danger dans la société. — Il a peut-être des secrets pour changer la vie? Non, il ne fait qu'en chercher, me répliquais-je. Enfin sa charité est ensorcelée, et j'en suis la prisonnière. Aucune autre âme n'aurait assez de force, — force de désespoir! — pour la supporter, — pour être protégée et aimée par lui. D'ailleurs, je ne me le figurais pas avec une autre âme: on voit son Ange, jamais l'Ange d'un autre, — je crois. J'étais dans son âme comme dans un palais qu'on a vidé pour ne pas voir une personne si peu noble que vous: voilà tout. Hélas! je dépendais bien de lui. Mais que voulait-il avec mon existence terne et lâche? Il ne me rendait pas meilleure,

" Je suis veuve... — J'étais veuve... — mais oui, j'ai été bien sérieuse jadis, et je ne suis pas née pour devenir squelette!... — Lui était presque un enfant... Ses délicatesses mystérieuses m'avaient séduite. J'ai oublié tout mon devoir humain pour le suivre. Quelle vie! La vraie vie est absente. Nous ne sommes pas au monde. Je vais où il va, il le faut. Et souvent il s'emporte contre moi, moi, la pauvre âme. Le Démon! — C'est un Démon, vous savez, ce n'est pas un homme.

"Il dit: "Je n'aime pas les femmes. L'amour est à réinventer, on le sait. Elles ne peuvent plus que vouloir un position assurée. La position gagnée, cœur et beauté sont mis de côté: il ne reste que froid dédain, l'aliment du mariage, aujourd'hui. Ou bien je vois des femmes, avec les signes du bonheur, dont, moi, j'aurais pu faire de bonnes camarades, dévorées tout d'abord par des brutes sensibles comme des bûchers..."

"Je l'écoute faisant de l'infamie une gloire, de la cruauté un charme: "Je suis de race lointaine: mes pères étaient Scandinaves: ils se perçaient les côtes, buvaient leur sang. — Je me ferai des entailles par tout le corps, je me tatouerai, je veux devenir hideux comme un Mongol: tu verras, je hurlerai dans les rues. Je veux devenir bien fou de rage. Ne me montre jamais de bijoux, je ramperais et me tordrais sur le tapis. Ma richesse, je la voudrais tachée de sang partout. Jamais je ne travaillerai..." Plusieurs nuits, son démon me saisissant, nous roulions, je luttais avec lui! — Les nuits, souvent, ivre, il se poste dans des rues ou dans des maisons, pour m'épouvanter mortellement. — "On me coupera vraiment le cou; ce sera dégoûtant. "Oh! ces jours où il veut marcher avec l'air du crime!

DÉLIRES

I

Vierge folle

L'Époux infernal

Écoutons, la confession d'un compagnon d'enfer:

"Ô divin Époux, mon Seigneur, ne refusez pas la confession de la plus triste de vos servantes. Je suis perdue. Je suis soûle. Je suis impure. Quelle vie!

"Pardon, divin Seigneur, pardon! Ah! pardon! Que de larmes! Et que de larmes encor plus tard, j'espère!

"Plus tard, je connaîtrai le divin Époux! Je suis née soumise à Lui. — L'autre peut me battre maintenant!

"À présent, je suis au fond du monde! Ô mes amies!... non, pas mes amies... Jamais délires ni tortures semblables... Est-ce bête!

"Ah! je souffre, je crie. Je souffre vraiment. Tout pourtant m'est permis, chargée du mépris des plus méprisables cœurs.

"Enfin, faisons cette confidence, quitte à la répéter vingt autres fois, — aussi morne, aussi insignifiante!

"Je suis esclave de l'Époux infernal, celui qui a perdu les vierges folles. C'est bien ce démon-là. Ce n'est pas un spectre, ce n'est pas un fantôme. Mais moi qui ai perdu la sagesse, qui suis damnée et morte au monde, — on ne me tuera pas! — Comment vous le décrire! Je ne sais même plus parler. Je suis en deuil, je pleure, j'ai peur. Un peu de fraîcheur, Seigneur, si vous voulez, si vous voulez bien!

J'ai tous les talents! — Il n'y a personne ici et il y a quelqu'un: je ne voudrais pas répandre mon trésor. — Veut-on des chants nègres, des danses de houris? Veut-on que je disparaisse, que je plonge à la recherche de l'anneau? Veut-on? Je ferai de l'or, des remèdes.

Fiez-vous donc à moi, la foi soulage, guide, guérit. Tous, venez, — même les petits enfants, — que je vous console, qu'on répande pour vous son cœur, — le cœur merveilleux! — Pauvres hommes, travailleurs! Je ne demande pas de prières; avec votre confiance seulement, je serai heureux.

— Et pensons à moi. Ceci me fait un peu regretter le monde. J'ai de la chance de ne pas souffrir plus. Ma vie ne fut que folies douces, c'est regrettable.

Bah! faisons toutes les grimaces imaginables.

Décidément, nous sommes hors du monde. Plus aucun son. Mon tact a disparu. Ah! mon château, ma Saxe, mon bois de saules. Les soirs, les matins, les nuits, les jours... Suis-je las!

Je devrais avoir mon enfer pour la colère, mon enfer pour l'orgueil, — et l'enfer de la caresse; un concert d'enfers.

Je meurs de lassitude. C'est le tombeau, je m'en vais aux vers, horreur de l'horreur! Satan, farceur, tu veux me dissoudre, avec tes charmes. Je réclame. Je réclame! un coup de fourche, une goutte de feu.

Ah! remonter à la vie! Jeter les yeux sur nos difformités. Et ce poison, ce baiser mille fois maudit! Ma faiblesse, la cruauté du monde! Mon Dieu, pitié, cachez-moi, je me tiens trop mal! — Je suis caché et je ne le suis pas.

C'est le feu qui se relève avec son damné.

arrêté, je suis prêt pour la perfection... Orgueil. — La peau de ma tête se dessèche. Pitié! Seigneur, j'ai peur. J'ai soif, si soif!

Ah! l'enfance, l'herbe, la pluie, le lac sur les pierres, le clair de lune quand le clocher sonnait douze... le diable est au clocher, à cette heure. Marie! Sainte Vierge!... — Horreur de ma bêtise.

Là-bas, ne sont-ce pas des âmes honnêtes, qui me veulent du bien... Venez... J'ai un oreiller sur la bouche, elles ne m'entendent pas, ce sont des fantômes. Puis, jamais personne ne pense à autrui. Qu'on n'approche pas. Je sens le roussi, c'est certain.

Les hallucinations sont innombrables. C'est bien ce que j'ai toujours eu: plus de foi en l'histoire, l'oubli des principes. Je m'en tairai: poètes et visionnaires seraient jaloux. Je suis mille fois le plus riche, soyons avare comme la mer.

Ah çà! l'horloge de la vie s'est arrêtée tout à l'heure. Je ne suis plus au monde. — La théologie est sérieuse, l'enfer est certainement en bas — et le ciel en haut. — Extase, cauchemar, sommeil dans un nid de flammes.

Que de malices, dans l'attention dans la campagne... Satan, Ferdinand, court avec les graines sauvages... Jésus marche sur les ronces purpurines, sans les courber... Jésus marchait sur les eaux irritées. La lanterne nous le montra debout, blanc et des tresses brunes, au flanc d'une vague d'émeraude...

Je vais dévoiler tous les mystères: mystères religieux ou naturels, mort, naissance, avenir, passé, cosmogonie, néant. Je suis maître en fantasmagories.

Écoutez!...

Nuit de l'enfer

J'ai avalé une fameuse gorgée de poison. — Trois fois béni soit le conseil qui m'est arrivé! — Les entrailles me brûlent. La violence du venin tord mes membres, me rend difforme, me terrasse. Je meurs de soif, j'étouffe, je ne puis crier. C'est l'enfer, l'éternelle peine! Voyez comme le feu se relève! Je brûle comme il faut. Va, démon!

J'avais entrevu la conversion au bien et au bonheur, le salut. Puis-je décrire la vision, l'air de l'enfer ne souffre pas les hymnes! C'était des millions de créatures charmantes, un suave concert spirituel, la force et la paix, les nobles ambitions, que sais-je?

Les nobles ambitions!

Et c'est encore la vie! — Si la damnation est éternelle! Un homme qui veut se mutiler est bien damné, n'est-ce pas? Je me crois en enfer, donc j'y suis. C'est l'exécution du catéchisme. Je suis esclave de mon baptême. Parents, vous avez fait mon malheur et vous avez fait le vôtre. Pauvre innocent! l'enfer ne peut attaquer les païens. — C'est la vie encore! Plus tard, les délices de la damnation seront plus profondes. Un crime, vite, que je tombe au néant, de par la loi humaine.

Tais-toi, mais tais-toi!... C'est la honte, le reproche, ici: Satan qui dit que le feu est ignoble, que ma colère est affreusement sotte. — Assez!... Des erreurs qu'on me souffle, magies, parfums faux, musiques puériles. — Et dire que je tiens la vérité, que je vois la justice: j'ai un jugement sain et

Farce continuelle! Mon innocence me ferait pleurer. La vie est la farce à mener par tous.

Assez! voici la punition. — En marche!

Ah! les poumons brûlent, les tempes grondent! la nuit roule dans mes yeux, par ce soleil! le cœur... les membres...

Où va-t-on? au combat? je suis faible! les autres avancent. Les outils, les armes... le temps!...

Feu! feu sur moi! Là! ou je me rends. — Lâches! — Je me tue! Je me jette aux pieds des chevaux!

Ah!...

— Je m'y habituerai.

Ce serait la vie française, le sentier de l'honneur!

Sauvez-les !

La raison est née. Le monde est bon. Je bénirai la vie. J'aimerai mes frères. Ce ne sont plus des promesses d'enfance. Ni l'espoir d'échapper à la vieillesse et à la mort. Dieu fait ma force, et je loue Dieu.

L'ennui n'est plus mon amour. Les rages, les débauches, la folie, dont je sais tous les élans et les désastres, — tout mon fardeau est déposé. Apprécions sans vertige l'étendu de mon innocence.

Je ne serais plus capable de demander le réconfort d'une bastonnade. Je ne me crois pas embarqué pour une noce avec Jésus-Christ pour beau-père.

Je ne suis pas prisonnier de ma raison. J'ai dit : Dieu. Je veux la liberté dans le salut : comment la poursuivre ? Les goûts frivoles m'ont quitté. Plus besoin de dévouement ni d'amour divin. Je ne regrette pas le siècle des cœurs sensibles. Chacun a sa raison, mépris et charité : je retiens ma place au sommet de cette angélique échelle de bon sens.

Quant au bonheur établi, domestique ou non... non, je ne peux pas. Je suis trop dissipé, trop faible. La vie fleurit par le travail, vieille vérité : moi, ma vie n'est pas assez pesante, elle s'envole et flotte loin au-dessus de l'action, ce cher point du monde.

Comme je deviens vieille fille, à manquer du courage d'aimer la mort !

Si Dieu m'accordait le calme céleste, aérien, la prière, — comme les anciens saints. — Les saints ! des forts ! les anachorètes, des artistes comme il n'en faut plus !

Connais-je encore la nature? me connais-je? — Plus de mots. J'ensevelis les morts dans mon ventre. Cris, tambour, danse, danse, danse, danse! Je ne vois même pas l'heure où, les blancs débarquant, je tomberai au néant.

Faim, soif, cris, danse, danse, danse, danse!

———

Les blancs débarquent. Le canon! Il faut se soumettre au baptême, s'habiller, travailler.

J'ai reçu au cœur le coup de la grâce. Ah! je ne l'avais pas prévu!

Je n'ai point fait le mal. Les jours vont m'être légers, le repentir me sera épargné. Je n'aurai pas eu les tourments de l'âme presque morte au bien, où remonte la lumière sévère comme les cierges funéraires. Le sort du fils de famille, cercueil prématuré couvert de limpides larmes. Sans doute la débauche est bête, le vice est bête; il faut jeter la pourriture à l'écart. Mais l'horloge ne sera pas arrivée à ne plus sonner que l'heure de la pure douleur! Vais-je être enlevé comme un enfant, pour jouer au paradis dans l'oubli de tout le malheur!

Vite! est-il d'autres vies? — Le sommeil dans la richesse est impossible. La richesse a toujours été bien public. L'amour divin seul octroie les clefs de la science.

Je vois que la nature n'est qu'un spectacle de bonté. Adieu chimères, idéals, erreurs.

Le chant raisonnable des anges s'élève du navire sauveur: c'est l'amour divin. — Deux amours! je puis mourir de l'amour terrestre, mourir de dévouement. J'ai laissé des âmes dont la peine s'accroîtra de mon départ! Vous me choisissez parmi les naufragés, ceux qui restent sont-ils pas mes amis?

force: te voilà, c'est la force. Tu ne sais ni où tu vas ni pourquoi tu vas, entre partout, réponds à tout. On ne te tuera pas plus que si tu étais cadavre." Au matin j'avais le regard si perdu et la contenance si morte, que ceux que j'ai rencontrés ne m'ont peut-être pas vu.

Dans les villes la boue m'apparaissait soudainement rouge et noire, comme une glace quand la lampe circule dans la chambre voisine, comme un trésor dans la forêt! Bonne chance, criais-je, et je voyais une mer de flammes et de fumées au ciel; et, à gauche, à droite, toutes les richesses flambant comme un milliard de tonnerres.

Mais l'orgie et la camaraderie des femmes m'étaient interdites. Pas même un compagnon. Je me voyais devant une foule exaspérée, en face du peloton d'exécution, pleurant du malheur qu'ils n'aient pu comprendre, et pardonnant! — Comme Jeanne d'Arc! — "Prêtres, professeurs, maîtres, vous vous trompez en me livrant à la justice. Je n'ai jamais été de ce peuple-ci; je n'ai jamais été chrétien; je suis de la race qui chantait dans le supplice; je ne comprends pas les lois; je n'ai pas le sens moral, je suis une brute: vous vous trompez..."

Oui, j'ai les yeux fermés à votre lumière. Je suis une bête, un nègre. Mais je puis être sauvé. Vous êtes de faux nègres, vous maniaques, féroces, avares. Marchand, tu es nègre; magistrat, tu es nègre; général, tu es nègre; empereur, vieille démangeaison, tu es nègre: tu as bu d'une liqueur non taxée, de la fabrique de Satan. — Ce peuple est inspiré par la fièvre et le cancer. Infirmes et vieillards sont tellement respectables qu'ils demandent à être bouillis. — Le plus malin est de quitter ce continent, où la folie rôde pour pourvoir d'otages ces misérables. J'entre au vrai royaume des enfants de Cham.

côté, dès l'âge de raison — qui monte au ciel, me bat, me renverse, me traîne.

La dernière innocence et la dernière timidité. C'est dit. Ne pas porter au monde mes dégoûts et mes trahisons.

Allons! La marche, le fardeau, le désert, l'ennui et la colère.

À qui me louer? Quelle bête faut-il adorer? Quelle sainte image attaque-t-on? Quels cœurs briserai-je? Quel mensonge dois-je tenir? — Dans quel sens marcher?

Plutôt, se garder de la justice. — La vie dure, l'abrutissement simple, — soulever, le poing desséché, le couvercle du cercueil, s'asseoir, s'étouffer. Ainsi point de vieillesse, ni de dangers: la terreur n'est pas française.

— Ah! je suis tellement délaissé que j'offre à n'importe quelle divine image des élans vers la perfection.

Ô mon abnégation, ô ma charité merveilleuse! ici-bas, pourtant!

De profundis Domine, suis-je bête!

Encore tout enfant, j'admirais le forçat intraitable sur qui se referme toujours le bagne; je visitais les auberges et les garnis qu'il aurait sacrés par son séjour; je voyais avec son idée le ciel bleu et le travail fleuri de la campagne; je flairais sa fatalité dans les villes. Il avait plus de force qu'un saint, plus de bon sens qu'un voyageur — et lui, lui seul! pour témoin de sa gloire et de sa raison.

Sur les routes, par des nuits d'hiver, sans gîte, sans habits, sans pain, une voix étreignait mon cœur gelé: "Faiblesse ou

La science, la nouvelle noblesse! Le progrès. Le monde marche! Pourquoi ne tournerait-il pas?

C'est la vision des nombres. Nous allons à l'Esprit. C'est très certain, c'est oracle, ce que je dis. Je comprends, et ne sachant m'expliquer sans paroles païennes, je voudrais me taire.

———

Le sang païen revient! L'Esprit est proche, pourquoi Christ ne m'aide-t-il pas, en donnant à mon âme noblesse et liberté. Hélas! l'Évangile a passé! l'Évangile! l'Évangile.

J'attends Dieu avec gourmandise. Je suis de race inférieure de toute éternité.

Me voici sur la plage armoricaine. Que les villes s'allument dans le soir. Ma journée est faite; je quitte l'Europe. L'air marin brûlera mes poumons; les climats perdus me tanneront. Nager, broyer l'herbe, chasser, fumer surtout; boire des liqueurs fortes comme du métal bouillant, — comme faisaient ces chers ancêtres autour des feux.

Je reviendrai, avec des membres de fer, la peau sombre, l'œil furieux: sur mon masque, on me jugera d'une race forte. J'aurai de l'or: je serai oisif et brutal. Les femmes soignent ces féroces infirmes retour des pays chauds. Je serai mêlé aux affaires politiques. Sauvé.

Maintenant je suis maudit, j'ai horreur de la patrie. Le meilleur, c'est un sommeil bien ivre, sur la grève.

———

On ne part pas. — Reprenons les chemins d'ici, chargé de mon vice, le vice qui a poussé ses racines de souffrance à mon

Il m'est bien évident que j'ai toujours été de race inférieure. Je ne puis comprendre la révolte. Ma race ne se souleva jamais que pour piller: tels les loups à la bête qu'ils n'ont pas tuée.

Je me rappelle l'histoire de la France fille aînée de l'Église. J'aurais fait, manant, le voyage de terre sainte, j'ai dans la tête des routes dans les plaines souabes, des vues de Byzance, des remparts de Solyme; le culte de Marie, l'attendrissement sur le crucifié s'éveillent en moi parmi les mille féeries profanes. — Je suis assis, lépreux, sur les pots cassés et les orties, au pied d'un mur rongé par le soleil. — Plus tard, reître, j'aurais bivaqué sous les nuits d'Allemagne.

Ah! encore: je danse le sabbat dans une rouge clairière, avec des vieilles et des enfants.

Je ne me souviens pas plus loin que cette terre-ci et le christianisme. Je n'en finirais pas de me revoir dans ce passé. Mais toujours seul; sans famille; même, quelle langue parlais-je? Je ne me vois jamais dans les conseils du Christ; ni dans les conseils des Seigneurs, — représentants du Christ.

Qu'étais-je au siècle dernier: je ne me retrouve qu'aujourd'hui. Plus de vagabonds, plus de guerres vagues. La race inférieure a tout couvert — le peuple, comme on dit, la raison; la nation et la science.

Oh! la science! On a tout repris. Pour le corps et pour l'âme, — le viatique, — on a la médecine et la philosophie, — les remèdes de bonnes femmes et les chansons populaires arrangées. Et les divertissements des princes et les jeux qu'ils interdisaient! Géographie, cosmographie, mécanique, chimie!...

Mauvais sang

J'ai de mes ancêtres gaulois l'œil bleu blanc, la cervelle étroite, et la maladresse dans la lutte. Je trouve mon habillement aussi barbare que le leur. Mais je ne beurre pas ma chevelure.

Les Gaulois étaient les écorcheurs de bêtes, les brûleurs d'herbes les plus ineptes de leur temps.

D'eux, j'ai: l'idolâtrie et l'amour du sacrilège; — oh! tous les vices, colère, luxure, — magnifique, la luxure; — surtout mensonge et paresse.

J'ai horreur de tous les métiers. Maîtres et ouvriers, tous paysans, ignobles. La main à plume vaut la main à charrue. — Quel siècle à mains! — Je n'aurai jamais ma main. Après, la domesticité mène trop loin. L'honnêteté de la mendicité me navre. Les criminels dégoûtent comme des châtrés: moi, je suis intact, et ça m'est égal.

Mais! qui a fait ma langue perfide tellement qu'elle ait guidé et sauvegardé jusqu'ici ma paresse? Sans me servir pour vivre même de mon corps, et plus oisif que le crapaud, j'ai vécu partout. Pas une famille d'Europe que je ne connaisse. — J'entends des familles comme la mienne, qui tiennent tout de la déclaration des Droits de l'Homme. — J'ai connu chaque fils de famille!

Si j'avais des antécédents à un point quelconque de l'histoire de France!

Mais non, rien.

Je parvins à faire s'évanouir dans mon esprit toute l'espérance humaine. Sur toute joie pour l'étrangler j'ai fait le bond sourd de la bête féroce.

J'ai appelé les bourreaux pour, en périssant, mordre la crosse de leurs fusils. J'ai appelé les fléaux, pour m'étouffer avec le sable, le sang. Le malheur a été mon dieu. Je me suis allongé dans la boue. Je me suis séché à l'air du crime. Et j'ai joué de bons tours à la folie.

Et le printemps m'a apporté l'affreux rire de l'idiot.

Or, tout dernièrement m'étant trouvé sur le point de faire le dernier couac! j'ai songé à rechercher la clef du festin ancien, où je reprendrais peut-être appétit.

La charité est cette clef. — Cette inspiration prouve que j'ai rêvé!

"Tu resteras hyène, etc...," se récrie le démon qui me couronna de si aimables pavots. "Gagne la mort avec tous tes appétits, et ton égoïsme et tous les péchés capitaux."

Ah! j'en ai trop pris: — Mais, cher Satan, je vous en conjure, une prunelle moins irritée! et en attendant les quelques petites lâchetés en retard, vous qui aimez dans l'écrivain l'absence des facultés descriptives ou instructives, je vous détache ces quelques hideux feuillets de mon carnet de damné.

UNE SAISON EN ENFER

Jadis, si je me souviens bien, ma vie était un festin où s'ouvraient tous les cœurs, où tous les vins coulaient. Un soir, j'ai assis la Beauté sur mes genoux. — Et je l'ai trouvée amère. — Et je l'ai injuriée.

Je me suis armé contre la justice.

Je me suis enfui. Ô sorcières, ô misère, ô haine, c'est à vous que mon trésor a été confié!

Le Poète se fait voyant par un long, immense et raisonné dérèglement de tous les sens.

Une Saison En Enfer

Arthur Rimbaud

www.ingramcontent.com/pod-product-compliance
Lightning Source LLC
Chambersburg PA
CBHW042118100526
44587CB00025B/4110